VALLEYS AND CANYONS

A TRUE BOOK

by

Larry Dane Brimner

Children's Press®
A Division of Grolier Publishing
New York London Hong Kong Sydney
Danbury, Connecticut

A valley below the
Himalayas in Tibet

Subject Consultant
Peter Goodwin
*Science Teacher, Kent School,
Kent, Connecticut*

Reading Consultant
Linda Cornwell
*Coordinator of School Quality
and Professional Improvement
Indiana State Teachers
Association*

Author's Dedication:
*For all my Happy Valley
Primary School friends*

Visit Children's Press® on the
Internet at:
http://publishing.grolier.com

*The photograph on the cover
shows the Grand Canyon. The
photograph on the title page
shows a river valley in Nepal.*

Library of Congress Cataloging-in-Publication Data

Brimner, Larry Dane
    Valleys and Canyons: a true book / by Larry Dane Brimner.
        p. cm. — (A true book)
    Includes bibliographical references and index.
    Summary: Describes different kinds of valleys and canyons and how
they are formed.
    ISBN 0-516-21569-8 (lib.bdg.)   0-516-27193-8 (pbk.)
    1. Valleys—Juvenile literature. 2. Canyons—Juvenile literature.
[1. Valleys. 2. Canyons.] I. Title. II. Series.
    GB561 .B75 2000
    551.44'2—dc21   99-058399
                                                                        CIP
                                                                         AC

GROLIER
PUBLISHING

Contents

A valley at Olympic National Park in Washington

Peaks and Valleys

From a soaring mountain peak, a hiker looks down upon a green valley. Wherever there are mountain peaks, there are valleys below them. Valleys are the low places between highlands, hills, or mountains.

The Earth has many kinds of valleys. They range from

Bryce Canyon in Utah

canyons and gorges to rift valleys and glacial valleys, as well as the valleys we know best—river valleys. Valleys are found on every continent, and even under the sea. Some valleys are wide and flat, with gently sloping sides. Others are deep and steep-sided gouges in the Earth. Why are valleys different from one another? Let's take a closer look and find out.

A glacial valley in Iceland

How Valleys Become Valleys

Scientists believe the rocky outer shell of the Earth "floats" on a layer of super-hot liquid rock called magma. This outer shell—the lithosphere—is not a solid chunk of rock, however. It is broken into eight major pieces, or

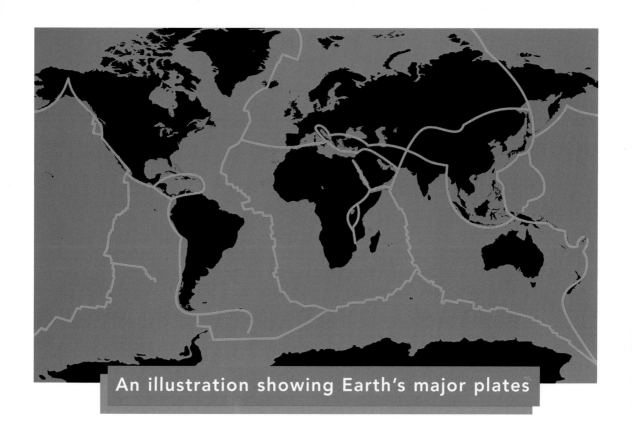

An illustration showing Earth's major plates

plates, and several smaller ones.

These plates are always in motion, but they move so slowly that we do not usually notice. Some of the world's

Valleys lie below folded mountains such as these in Alberta, Canada.

mountains were formed when these plates pushed against each other, causing great waves of rock to rise above the sur- rounding land. Such mountains are called folded mountains. The areas next to these moun- tains that were not pushed up became valleys.

As Earth's plates have moved, they have made long cracks, or faults, in the Earth's crust. Huge blocks of rock on either side of the faults may push up or slip

As the Earth's plates move, huge blocks of rock may push up or slip down.

down, forming fault-block mountains. Many of the mountains in western North America were formed this way. The basins, or hollows, next to the faults formed valleys.

A valley below the Grand Tetons, a fault-block mountain range in Wyoming

A valley below Mount Ararat,
a volcanic mountain in Turkey

Mountains also formed when magma pushed under the Earth's crust to form large domes. The magma then exploded out of openings, or vents, in the lithosphere to form volcanoes. The lowlands surrounding these volcanic mountains became valleys.

Valleys are always connected to the hills and mountains that border them. But other forces also help to form and shape valleys.

River Valleys

The classic valley begins when rain falls. It flows down the hill-sides and into a channel. There, it forms a river and follows the shortest, easiest path to the sea.

The river cuts away at the bottom of the channel and makes it deeper. The fine sand, or sediment, at the bottom of

A river valley in Colorado

the channel mixes with the water and is carried away. Later, this sediment drops out of the water and settles where the river ends.

If the river were the only force wearing away, or eroding, the land, it would cut a deep gash with straight up-and-down sides. However, other elements—such as rain and frost—are wearing away the sides of the channel while the river is cutting it deeper. These other elements work to slope the sides and form a wide, V-shaped valley.

Eventually, the sides will be worn flat and the valley becomes a broad plain like the

The Mississippi River Valley in Mississippi

Mississippi River Valley. Then the river will no longer rush downhill. Instead, it will flow sluggishly to the sea.

Glacial Valleys

At many times during Earth's history, the climate has been much colder than it is now. During these cold spells, or ice ages, ice stretched down from the polar regions to cover large areas of the planet. The great weight of the ice made it flow like a slow-moving river.

A modern-day glacier in Alaska

These rivers of ice, or glaciers, were like giant bulldozers.
As they pushed downhill, they
plucked huge boulders from

In many parts of the world, huge valleys have been carved out by glaciers.

the ground and carved out deep valleys.

Glacial valleys aren't V-shaped like the valleys cut by rivers. Instead, they are shaped like the letter U. This is because glaciers eroded the sides as well as the bottoms of their rocky, ice-filled channels.

Glacial valleys are U-shaped, not V-shaped.

Some glacial valleys have been filled by fjords.

When the ice age ended and Earth warmed, the glaciers melted. The melting ice then raised the levels of the oceans. This caused glacial valleys along the coasts to fill with seawater, which created fjords, or inlets. Some fjords are more than 4,000 feet (1,219 meters) deep!

Glaciers are active today, but only in places where it is very cold. These glaciers are busy carving valleys of their own, just like the glaciers of long ago.

Rift Valleys

Rift valleys, which are also called grabens, are not made by erosion. They are made by faulting action—the movement of Earth's plates. Rift valleys occur between faults that are parallel to each other. When the plates move apart, the ground between the faults slips down to form valleys.

The Great Rift Valley in Africa

Africa's Great Rift Valley is the largest rift valley on any of the large landmasses we call continents. It is about 4,036 miles (6,458 kilometers) long and drops far below sea level.

A rift valley in Israel

Scientists think the Great Rift Valley is continuing to form. Some of them believe that in millions of years it may split eastern Africa off from the rest of Africa to form a new continent.

Gorges

Water is one of nature's most powerful tools. Frozen water can chip away rock and bulldoze deep glacial valleys. As a liquid, water can shape river valleys and fill them with rich sediment that is ideal for growing crops. But water is also responsible for much erosion beneath the Earth's surface.

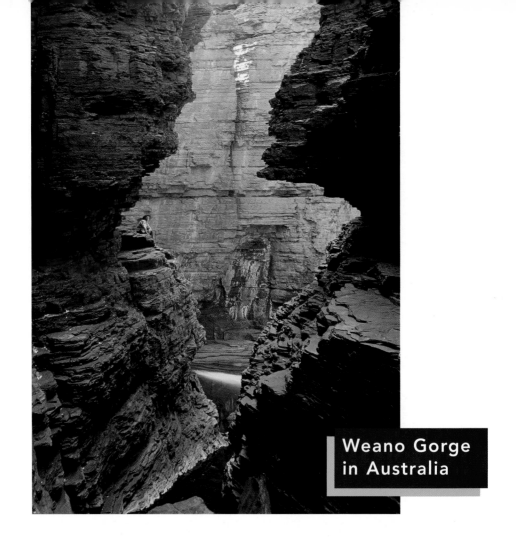

Weano Gorge
in Australia

As rain falls to Earth, it picks
up a gas called carbon dioxide. This is the gas that people
and animals breathe out. It is

also the gas given off by dead and decaying plants. So, as the rain seeps into the soil, it picks up even more carbon dioxide. The rain and carbon dioxide mix together to make carbonic acid.

Over millions of years, this acid is able to dissolve lime-stone, a soft rock made from the tightly-packed skeletons of tiny sea creatures. Eventually, however, the acid water drains away and air enters the hollow

A limestone cave

left behind. An underground cave has been made.

It may remain a cave for a very long time, but rainwater continues to trickle through its roof. Eventually, the roof may

The Flume, a gorge
in New Hampshire

grow weak and crumble. Now
the cave has become a gorge.
   The term "gorge" may be
used to describe any small,
narrow canyon with steep sides,
but it often refers to those

places formed from collapsed caves. Sometimes, a natural stone bridge may arch across the gorge. Once, the bridge may have formed part of a cave's roof. Now it links one side of the gorge with the other.

Canyons

Canyons are valleys formed by river erosion, but they are different from classic river valleys. Why? Classic river valleys have sloping sides because rain and frost have worn them away. Canyons have steep sides because they form in dry, or arid, places where

Canyon de Chelly,
Arizona

there is little rainfall to wear
down the sides.

Canyons are a lot like gorges,
but there are some differences.
Gorges have straight up-and-
down, or vertical, sides, while

the sides of canyons are usually stepped. This is because the little rain that falls in a canyon comes suddenly and all at once. So canyon rivers—and their power to erode—tend to rise and fall

Devil Canyon, Montana

Bryce Canyon, Utah

with these sudden storms. Also, as a river cuts through a canyon, it runs into different layers of rock. Some of these layers are softer than others, and are more easily eroded away.

The Grand Canyon

The Grand Canyon is one of North America's most notable features. Cut by the Colorado River, it is 5 to 6 million years old and, at its deepest point, about 6,000 ft. (1,829 m) deep.

Submarine Valleys

Valleys that lie under the surface of the ocean are said to be submarine valleys. These seafloor valleys have some of the most rugged features found anywhere on Earth.

Many submarine valleys probably were formed when the seas held less water. Glaciers and rivers

A map showing submarine valleys along North America and South America

may have eroded these valleys during ice ages of long ago. When the ice melted and the seas rose, the valleys were covered by water and became submarine valleys.

We also know that faulting action has created deep canyons where Earth's plates are being pulled apart under the sea. One such rift—the largest anywhere on Earth—is bigger than the Great Rift Valley, and it is getting bigger all the time. The Great Global Rift runs along the 40,000-mile- (64,000-km-) long mid-ocean mountain system under the major oceans of the world. But scientists cannot yet explain how all submarine valleys and canyons formed.

Canyonlands and the Green River in Utah

Whether on land or under the sea, valleys are never finished. Water and ice—and even wind—wear them down continually. The constant movement of Earth's plates is hard at work too. These forces are a reminder that our Earth is always changing.

To Find Out More

Here are some additional resources to help you learn more about valleys and canyons:

 **Books**

Parker, Steve, and Parker, Jane. **Mountains and Valleys.** Silver Dolphin, 1996.

Pope, Joyce. **The Children's Atlas of Natural Wonders.** Millbrook Press, 1995.

Rothaus, Don P. **Canyons** (Biomes of Nature Series). Child's World, 1996.

Sattler, Helen Roney. **Our Patchwork Planet: The Story of Plate Tectonics.** Lothrop, Lee & Shepard, 1995.

Sauvain, Philip Arthur. **Rivers and Valleys** (Geography Detective). Carolrhoda Books, 1996.

Organizations and Online Sites

Canadian Rockies Panoramas

http://GeoImages.Berkeley. EDU/GeoImages/QTVR/ CanadianRockies/Canadian Rockies.html

Amazing virtual-reality images of this beautiful mountain range and its valleys.

National Geographic Society at the Grand Canyon

http://www. nationalgeographic.com/ media/books/grandcanyon/ index.html

Images, an interactive map, and facts and features of the Grand Canyon.

Plate Tectonics

http://www.cotf.edu/ete/ modules/msese/ earthsysflr/plates1.html

A site explaining how movements of the Earth's plates affect land and sea.

Important Words

channel long groove or furrow

climate average weather conditions of a place over a period of years

continent one of Earth's major land areas

decaying rotting, breaking apart

eroded wore away

gouges scoops out

highlands high or hilly country

ice age period in Earth's history when large areas of land were covered by ice sheets

parallel lying in the same direction but always the same distance apart

polar having to do with the North or South Pole

sluggishly slowly

Index

Meet the Author

Larry Dane Brimner is the author of more than sixty books for children. For Children's Press, he has written books on many different topics, including *The World Wide Web*, *Cockroaches*, and *Caves*. Larry grew up in a valley, but now divides his time between a house on a mountain (Rico, Colorado) and one on a mesa (San Diego, California).